Nine Months

*with*

God and Your Baby

ÉLINE LANDON

Translated by James Henri McMurtrie

# Nine Months
## *with*
# God and Your Baby

### Spiritual Preparation for Birth

SOPHIA INSTITUTE PRESS

Manchester, New Hampshire

Sophia Institute Press
Box 5284, Manchester, NH 03108
1-800-888-9344

www.SophiaInstitute.com

Sophia Institute Press® is a registered trademark of Sophia Institute.

**Library of Congress Cataloging-in-Publication Data**

To come.

First printing

*To Philéas, who was the first one*
*to allow me to be a mother.*
*To Théophane, who helped me enlarge my heart.*
*To Emonah, who opened up a peaceful path in me*
*and who allowed these meditations to come forth*
*by her presence in my womb.*

# Contents

# Preface

When I was expecting my first child, I was surprised by all that needed to be done to prepare for the birth. In preparing for childbirth, well-informed women who do not find what suits them are rare. In addition to the classic maternity preparations, we can choose haptonomy, prenatal yoga, sophrology, pool preparations, the Bonapace Method, and so many other things that the general public still does not know. There are many opportunities to prepare for the great moment of a baby's arrival in the world. These opportunities allow each couple to find what they are looking for, enabling them to be fully ready to help their child to be born and assisting in alleviating labor pains.

Nonetheless, the spiritual welcoming of the child, which prepares us for the sacred presence of a new being in us, seems to be lacking. The word "pregnancy" would make us believe that what is going on in us is simply getting fat! How can we communicate about this state, which is so much more than that and completely overwhelms us?

By welcoming life in us, we participate in God's work of creation. The birth of a new being is a sacred mystery, and it seems vital to me to prepare for it by meditating on biblical texts and praying.

While I was expecting my third child, the idea of this meditation grew in me, and this book gradually took form. Thus, I offer you these scriptural passages that relate to the conception of a child, his presence in his mother's body for nine months, and his arrival among us. In each chapter, you will find a pregnancy-related theme, a biblical text, a meditative commentary on that text, a suggestion for further reflection, and a prayer.

This book is to be read month after month; it is not intended to be read all at once. It is necessary to take the time to live this mystery fully and gradually.

We can schedule a time when we will not be disturbed as we read and pray. We can delve into the meditation throughout the month with complementary passages on the same subject before we go on to the next theme. Prayer is equally important. We can settle into a calm, pleasant place, light a candle, and put ourselves in God's presence with the aid of a simple prayer, such as "Here I am, Lord."

These proposals are starting points. Do not hesitate to let yourself be led by the Holy Spirit so that your own prayer can spring up.

This work is intended more for the woman who is carrying the child who will come into the world. Nonetheless, the man should not feel left out. The couple's communication is basic, and these meditations can serve as a basis for exchanges between the couple. The father can find material that will supply his reflections and prayers about the coming of his child. Moreover, a prayer is offered for the father to say in the chapter "The Reception of the Child."

Bringing a child into the world makes us the latest members of a group. In becoming mothers, we join a host of women with their joys and wounds. Our own history and our relationship with our mothers will affect our pregnancy, a period during which we are extremely sensitive. We are more receptive and more open to our emotions. Let us take our place in this new group and allow ourselves time to enter into it.

Month after month, let us ask the Lord to prepare us for welcoming the life that is soon to be or is already present in us.

Nine Months

*with*

God and Your Baby

# The Desire for a Child

So it went on year by year; as often as she went up to the house of the LORD, she used to provoke her. Therefore Hannah wept and would not eat. And Elkanah, her husband, said to her, "Hannah, why do you weep? And why do you not eat? And why is your heart sad? Am I not more to you than ten sons?"

After they had eaten and drunk in Shiloh, Hannah rose. Now Eli the priest was sitting on the seat beside the doorpost of the temple of the LORD. She was deeply distressed and prayed to the LORD, and wept bitterly. And she vowed a vow and said, "O LORD of hosts, if thou wilt indeed look on the affliction of thy maidservant, and remember me, and not forget thy maidservant, but wilt give to thy maidservant a son, then I will give him to the LORD all the days of his life, and no razor shall touch his head."

As she continued praying before the LORD, Eli observed her mouth. Hannah was speaking in her heart; only her lips moved, and her voice was not heard;

*therefore Eli took her to be a drunken woman. And Eli said to her, "How long will you be drunken? Put away your wine from you." But Hannah answered, "No, my lord, I am a woman sorely troubled; I have drunk neither wine nor strong drink, but I have been pouring out my soul before the LORD. Do not regard your maidservant as a base woman, for all along I have been speaking out of my great anxiety and vexation." Then Eli answered, "Go in peace, and the God of Israel grant your petition which you have made to him." And she said, "Let your maidservant find favor in your eyes." Then the woman went her way and ate, and her countenance was no longer sad. (1 Sam. 1:7–18)*

Hannah is one of the women in the Bible who was not able to bear a child until she reached old age.

Each year, Hannah goes to the sanctuary to plead with the Lord. Because this desire for a child is not satisfied, her shame torments her. She is "sorely troubled," "deeply distressed," "weeping bitterly," and "her heart is sad." We can look at Hannah's despair and the powerlessness of her husband, who responds: "Am I not more to you than ten sons?" He also would like to satisfy her, but it is impossible because she is awaiting someone else, and the conjugal bond is not enough to fulfill her. Waiting for a child implies a couple—a man and a woman. This desire lives in both the man and the woman, even if we do not know how to express it in the same way and at the same time. Seeing Hannah's sadness also afflicts her husband, who would very much like to make her happy.

We do not all experience this profound sadness, but, in Hannah's despair and prayer, there is a teaching for each and every situation. The call to maternity is sometimes so strong that it is not hard for us to imagine what Hannah can be feeling. And when one is waiting for a child, it is not hard to be like her, begging the Lord to intervene in our favor. We should not neglect the prayer of intercession, which can be very powerful.

Let us look at Hannah's determination, which enables her to release her sadness. She goes up. She willingly pours her heart out to God. The text tells us that she "prayed to the LORD and wept bitterly," and again, "She continued praying before the LORD," and again, she spoke "in her heart." These phrases emphasize that prayer is not optional but is the heart of the matter. The prayer sustains Hannah's waiting; she is full of hope. After her prayer of supplication, it is said that "her countenance was no longer sad." Hannah finds peace again. She goes away and agrees to eat and to get back to living. She does not yet know that she is going to conceive; nonetheless, she does not feel sad, as she did before. The prayer and the exchange with Eli, which is first turbulent and then filled with compassion, changes her heart. She can peacefully go back to her family. Her face changes, even though the circumstances are apparently the same.

Hannah teaches us, through this, to pray and not to scorn our heart's desires. Even if our fertility has not been tested, we should be attentive to our desire for a child and entrust it to

God in prayer. Even before the conception of our children, we need to pray. Like Hannah, we should live in confidence and surrender, handing everything over into God's hands.

Hannah's prayer certainly expresses all that she is experiencing. She is in the Temple to "pour out her soul before the LORD," and she "is speaking in her heart," to the extent that Eli, the high priest, thinks that she is drunk. "For all along I have been speaking out of my great anxiety and vexation." Let us also allow our hearts to overflow before the Lord in prayer and not hesitate to entrust our pain, joys, fears, hope, and sometimes even our anger to Him. Hannah does not worry about what people will say. She does not look around her to see if people are observing her; she lets her heart speak. So, if tears overwhelm us, let them flow without shame.

God is not distant. He wants to be close to us, and we can, with complete confidence, confide in Him, by way of heartfelt prayer that overflows and expresses who we are in the depths of our being. It allows us to make things right. The child who will be entrusted to us is a gift and not a duty. Hannah affirms this by telling the Lord that if He will "give to thy maidservant a son, then I will give him to the LORD all the days of his life." The child is no longer only her child but becomes the Lord's child.

When Eli understands Hannah's approach, he blesses her, saying, "Go in peace, and the God of Israel grant your petition which you have made to him." We can also understand that this "go in peace" is for us. Our heart stops being agitated. We see very well how Hannah's attitude changes. We perceive the turmoil that shakes her whole being and ends up subsiding, which leads her to be much more peaceful.

Therefore, let us also walk peacefully and confidently as we carry out the plan that God has for us. Let us know how to express our requests with the certainty that what God gives us is more than we can hope for. This verse can accompany us while we are waiting:

Take delight in the LORD,
and he will give you the desires of your heart.
Commit your way to the LORD;
trust in him, and he will act. (Ps. 37:4–5)

*For Further Reflection*

During this month, we can also meditate on the story of Elizabeth, the mother of John the Baptist (Luke 1:5–25). It is quite similar to Hannah's. It is also like the story of Abraham and Sarah, when the angel tells Sarah that she will have a son in her old age (Gen. 18:1–15). We can meditate on Sarah's disbelief and on the fulfillment of God's promise to this couple, which is beyond anything that is humanly possible. Let us look at the desire that is in the hearts of these women.

## A Concluding Prayer

*Yes, Lord, You understand the desires of my heart.
You know the desire that is in me, that is in us — to
be able to receive and welcome a child in myself. May
he be Your gift. I entrust all my joys and sorrows and
hopes to You — like Hannah, who was not afraid to
show her despair in the sanctuary. She knew that You
would hear her prayer and that she could express it
to You in the depths of her heart. Lord, give me hope
while I'm waiting, and help me to pray to You with
complete confidence. Amen.*

# The Conception of a Child

*Then Tobias exhorted the virgin, and said to her: "Sarah, arise, and let us pray to God to day, and tomorrow, and the next day: because for these three nights we are joined to God: and when the third night is over, we will be in our own wedlock. For we are the children of saints, and we must not be joined together like heathens that know not God."*

*So they both arose, and prayed earnestly both together that health might be given them, and Tobias said: "Lord God of our father, may the heavens and the earth, and the sea, and the fountains, and the rivers, and all thy creatures that are in them, bless thee. Thou madest Adam of the slime of the earth, and gavest him Eve for a helper. And now, Lord, thou knowest, that not for fleshly lust do I take my sister to wife, but only for the love of posterity, in which thy name may be blessed for ever and ever."*

*Sarah also said: "Have mercy on us, O Lord, have mercy on us, and let us grow old both together in health." (see Tob. 8:4–10, Douay-Rheims)*

Here is the story of two young people, Tobias and Sarah. Sarah is in the grip of a terrible misfortune. She has had seven husbands, all of whom died on the night of their wedding. When Tobias tells Sarah's parents that he intends to marry their daughter, everyone fears for his life. Tobias's tomb is dug even before his death! But Tobias trusts God. Before going to sleep on their wedding night, both young spouses get up to pray, "Sister, arise, and let us pray to God today, and tomorrow, and the next day."

The spouses' prayer is basic. It confronts us with the mystery of the creation of man and woman and their descendants. We can praise God for our union and beg Him to supply us with His grace and protection.

Even before the arrival of a child, the couple comes first. The couple's solidarity is necessary for the growth of a child. We should not neglect to pray together and to be open to the grace that was received during the marriage ceremony when God Himself joined us. We should be united to each other, in God. We should praise God for this creative work and for the love that unites us. This love allows us to receive each other as a gift and reminds us of the promise we gave each other: "I receive you as my spouse, and I give myself to you."

This is the will of God, who said at creation that "a man leaves his father and his mother and cleaves to his wife, and they become one flesh" (Gen. 2:24). The time from the desire for a child to the moment of conception can be long. Nonetheless, entrusting our lives to each other, which can lead to the creation of a new life, is a source of hope. May this union of bodies and hearts, which God wants, be blessed so that new life may spring up in Him. We should pray, like Tobias and Sarah, for our life as a couple.

One translation of this passage introduces the prayer of a couple in another way. Tobias says to Sarah, "Arise, and let us pray." Tobias calls Sarah "my sister," and in his prayer he says, in reference to Adam, that God "gavest him Eve for a helper." The other version adds "and to sustain him" and "I will make him a helper that he will have as a partner." Here, we can meditate on the grace that the woman has by virtue of being a woman. This helper that Tobias talks about, in reference to the Genesis account, is sometimes poorly understood, as if the woman were created only in reference to the man and not to herself. Man and woman are inseparable.

They were created in God's image and receive each other as a gift of God.

In her book *Oser vivre l'amour* (Dare to live love),[1] Georgette Blaquière, a mother and a theologian, speaking of the charism of the woman, insists that the woman, before being the sexual partner, is first the sister. The man and the woman recognize each other as unique; each has inherent worth. The woman is the man's sister; each one comes from the same Father. She stands opposite the man and is his free and equal partner and companion. The woman gives life; she can give it in a biological manner but also in a spiritual and mystical one. It is possible to give birth to men in many ways by "putting them in God's world," to use Blaquière's expression.

Are we aware of the beauty of the woman's vocation? Do we thank God for the grace He gives us? We can sometimes feel the burden that was carried by the women of our families' past generations and fear what our own femininity may imply. God wanted men and women to

---

[1] Georgette Blaquière, *Oser vivre l'amour* (Nouan-Le-Fuzelier, France: Editions des Béatitudes, 1994), 35–37.

pursue His work of creation. He wants us to be free. And that is good.

Tobias prays by calling the Lord the "God of our father," and he speaks of his desire to create a family that will bless God's name forever and ever. In this way, he places himself in a string of generations that follow each other.

Each of us has a history. We have parents, who themselves have parents, who have parents, and so forth. And, in turn, we will become parents! The union of two partners creates a new life that will then be in a line of descent. The welcoming of a child is done by the whole family, which has already experienced many happy and unhappy events. Being pregnant often brings buried emotions to the surface. This includes emotions dealing with how our families welcomed us when we were small. We can entrust to the Lord our families, parents, and in-laws, who will also be welcoming this child. We should ask God to heal the wounds in the families who gave life to us and to bless them.

*For Further Reflection*

We can meditate on the mystery of the creation of man and woman (Gen. 2:18–25), as Tobias invites us to do in his prayer, and allow ourselves to be permeated with the plan of God, who created man and woman in His image. We can contemplate the sleep of Adam, who does not know what God is preparing for him. Then, let us hear Adam's cry of admiration when he discovers the woman, who is similar to, yet different from him: "This at last is bone of my bones / and flesh of my flesh." Let us attach ourselves to the last verses: "Therefore a man leaves his father and his mother and cleaves to his wife, and they become one flesh. And the man and his wife were both naked, and were not ashamed."

## A Concluding Prayer

*Lord, blessed are You for creating man and woman, Your creation. Blessed are You for the love that unites us to each other. May our union be a communion, and may it reinforce our unity. Look at our sincere hearts, and help us turn toward each other. Therefore, Lord, allow this baby to be born, and may my heart welcome him. We entrust our families to You and pray that You would bless them in their joys as well as in their sorrows. Heal that which is wounded in them. Amen.*

*First Month*

# The Annunciation

*In the sixth month the angel Gabriel was sent from God to a city of Galilee named Nazareth, to a virgin betrothed to a man whose name was Joseph, of the house of David; and the virgin's name was Mary. And he came to her and said, "Hail, full of grace, the Lord is with you!" But she was greatly troubled at the saying, and considered in her mind what sort of greeting this might be. And the angel said to her, "Do not be afraid, Mary, for you have found favor with God. And behold, you will conceive in your womb and bear a son, and you shall call his name Jesus.*

*He will be great, and will be called the Son of the Most High; and the Lord God will give to him the throne of his father David, and he will reign over the house of Jacob for ever; and of his kingdom there will be no end."*

*And Mary said to the angel, "How can this be, since I have no husband?" And the angel said to her,*

*"The Holy Spirit will come upon you, and the power of the Most High will overshadow you; therefore the child to be born will be called holy, the Son of God.*

*And behold, your kinswoman Elizabeth in her old age has also conceived a son; and this is the sixth month with her who was called barren. For with God nothing will be impossible."*

*And Mary said, "Behold, I am the handmaid of the Lord; let it be to me according to your word." And the angel departed from her. (Luke 1:26–38)*

The moment of the discovery and announcement of a pregnancy is unique. We wait, we hope, and we feel it; there he is — a new being is in the process of being formed in us! According to the circumstances, we can feel very joyful or disturbed. The feelings and perceptions are sometimes mixed. At this stage, we can contemplate Mary, to whom the angel announces that she will bear a child, who will be conceived by the Holy Spirit.

First, the angel invites Mary to rejoice: "Hail Mary, full of grace, the Lord is with you." The salutation of the angel appears in another translation in this way, "Rejoice, Mary, the Lord has granted you a special grace." This first word of the angel to Mary is joyous. Mary is the chosen one; she is "full of grace." This gift that the Lord offers through her to all people produces profound joy. God joins man; He makes Himself flesh in Mary; and He is Emmanuel, "God with us." This mystery is so great that we are called to contemplate it, meditate on it, and allow it to permeate us. How joyful Mary is to be the Mother of the Savior!

But Scripture then tells us that Mary was overwhelmed. The angel's unique greeting disturbs her. She is not immediately full of joy, and she does not become ecstatic before this vision of an angel of God. She does not get mixed up in words of thanks and praise. No, Mary wonders what this means, and she is full of fear.

So, we must understand this sentence: "Do not be afraid, Mary, for you have found favor with God." The angel Gabriel invites Mary to be confident and points her toward God's omnipotence in response to her question, "How can this be?" He says, "The Holy Spirit will come upon you, and the power of the Most High will overshadow you." So, why should she continue to be afraid?

The Holy Spirit comes into Mary and completely enfolds her. And Mary humbly accepts the angel's announcement with this word that is full of strength and wisdom: "Let it be to me according to your word." It is simple. Mary says yes to the most extraordinary of things. God is made flesh in her. She does not ask any more questions and does not argue. She surrenders. Mary's assent to this incredible miracle invites us, in turn, to say yes to that which is happening in us. We wanted these children, or they invited themselves into our wombs. In any case, we are to consent to this new life by fully welcoming it.

So, we should welcome this announcement that these new beings are growing in us and allowing us to be enfolded in God's omnipotence, as was the case with Mary. In confronting all the qualms as well as all the joys that are in us, let us surrender and totally entrust ourselves to the Father's will. We can fearlessly let ourselves be led into this new maternal adventure.

We do not, of course, know where we are going. But did Mary know? Could she imagine what her life would be like? How would Joseph react?

But the Lord also takes care of this question. He has not left Mary alone to face what has just happened. Joseph, who wanted to repudiate her in secret, sees an angel, who tells him in a dream not to be afraid to take Mary as his wife. Thus, he stays with her, watches over her and the child, and is alerted as soon as danger threatens their lives. God does not go away after His work starts. He accompanies Mary and Joseph all the way, and, in the same way, He will accompany us.

We should also allow ourselves to be "interrupted" in our everyday lives. The angel enters Mary's home and goes to where she is, which is probably in the midst of her usual work—the extraordinary amid the ordinary. The arrival of these little beings in our wombs is not noisy. They arrive and grow while we continue with our life, work, and activities. We do not even yet suspect that they are present, that their cells are multiplying, and that their hearts start to beat in the third week of their lives! Who could imagine what goes on in our bodies? We do not see any of it.

Let us listen to the parable of Jesus, who speaks to us in these words about the sower:

> The kingdom of God is as if a man should scatter seed upon the ground, and should sleep and rise night and day, and the seed should sprout and grow, he knows not how. The earth produces of itself, first the blade, then the ear, then the full grain in the ear. But when the grain is ripe, at once he puts in the sickle, because the harvest has come. (Mark 4:26–29)

We do not really know how this miracle takes place in us, and yet, without our being aware of it, our little ones are growing in us. The exchange of words between the angel and Mary is brief; it is directed toward the most important thing and is full of silence. In fact, it is in silence that we can truly and naturally meet God. In silence, we can really be ourselves without worrying about what our neighbor thinks. It is in this silence that we can welcome the presence of our children in us and that God works to make them grow.

God works marvels in the midst of our most ordinary daily lives. So, let us allow the Lord to call us, as He called Mary, to joy, confidence, and humility in the face of the greatness of the miracle that is in us.

*For Further Reflection*

We can read Psalm 127, inviting the Lord to act in us in order to establish a solid foundation in our family. Let us meditate on the meaning of the first verse: "Unless the LORD builds the house, those who build it labor in vain." We undoubtedly want to build our house on rock so that no storm can destroy it. Our rock is the Lord. Let us allow Him to build our household.

And let us allow verse 3 to resonate in us: "Lo, sons are a heritage from the LORD, the fruit of the womb a reward." It is an invitation to measure the gift the Lord gives us by entrusting these precious children into our hands. They are the real treasures of the family.

## A Concluding Prayer

*Lord, blessed are You for the announcement of this new life that is developing in me. I entrust to You my feelings of joy but also my fear of change and disruptions. Give me the grace of confidence so that I may not be fearful anymore. Like Mary, let my yes be a real yes, a free and humble one—yes to life, yes to the child whom I already bear. Come live in me. Amen.*

*Second Month*

# Creation of God

O LORD, thou hast searched me and known me!
Thou knowest when I sit down and when I rise up;
   thou discernest my thoughts from afar.
Thou searchest out my path and my lying down,
   and art acquainted with all my ways.
Even before a word is on my tongue,
   lo, O LORD, thou knowest it altogether.
Thou dost beset me behind and before,
   and layest thy hand upon me.
Such knowledge is too wonderful for me;
   it is high, I cannot attain it.

Whither shall I go from thy Spirit?
   Or whither shall I flee from thy presence?
If I ascend to heaven, thou art there!
   If I make my bed in Sheol, thou art there!
If I take the wings of the morning
   and dwell in the uttermost parts of the sea,
even there thy hand shall lead me,
   and thy right hand shall hold me.

*If I say, "Let only darkness cover me,*
   *and the light about me be night,"*
*even the darkness is not dark to thee,*
   *the night is bright as the day;*
   *for darkness is as light with thee.*

*For thou didst form my inward parts,*
   *thou didst knit me together in my mother's womb.*
*I praise thee, for thou art fearful and wonderful.*
   *Wonderful are thy works!*
*Thou knowest me right well;*
   *my frame was not hidden from thee,*
*when I was being made in secret,*
   *intricately wrought in the depths of the earth.*
*Thy eyes beheld my unformed substance;*
   *in thy book were written, every one of them,*
*the days that were formed for me,*
   *when as yet there was none of them.*
*How precious to me are thy thoughts, O God!*
   *How vast is the sum of them!*
*If I would count them, they are more than the sand.*
   *When I awake, I am still with thee. (Ps. 139:1–18)*

How we marvel at this Creator God, who knows us in such a total and perfect way! We can even be frightened by the first verses: "Thou knowest when I sit down and when I rise up; thou discernest my thoughts from afar." God certainly knows us better than we know ourselves. In fact, He is the one who made us, and this is what allows us to call him our Father. We are once again faced with the mystery of creation: even before we were born of a father and a mother, we existed in God, who knows everything about us and wants us. Nothing can escape Him. His gaze goes to the depths of our hearts.

This psalm tells us that God knit us together in our mothers' wombs and that we were made in secret. He silently and patiently knit us together. God's work is not noisy or hurried. It acts calmly, without our even perceiving it. We are hardly aware that persons are being formed inside us, and nonetheless God already knows it. Not only does He know it, but, regarding each person, "in thy book were written ... the days that were formed for [him], /

when as yet there was none of them". This is enough to make us dizzy. We can, with the psalmist, proclaim, "How precious to me are thy thoughts, O God! / How vast is the sum of them!"

Each of us is unique. Even twins are very different, despite their apparent similarities.

Let us marvel, like the psalmist, when faced with the way life grows. From the start of this new stage of life, let us praise the Lord for what He sees that we do not yet see. These beings have not yet been formed; God sees them as the beings they will become. He creates and shapes them. He loves them infinitely, as the unique beings they already are. Even babies who are not able to see the light of day are loved and wanted by God as special people.

Before existing within us, our babies existed in the heart of the Creator of everything. We should infinitely respect these unique babies, who are, for now, hidden in us, and we should be open to the mystery that is in them.

Today, thanks to modern technologies, it is easy to know the baby's sex, sometimes even from the first ultrasound. Let us not hurry. We should take our time without scanning the screen during the tests. Our babies are there, hidden in our wombs. There will come a time when they will be revealed to us. Each couple is free to ask about the sex of their child. Some people prefer to know it so as to prepare better for his arrival, name him, and have him take his place in the family. Others want to wait for the moment of birth and their first face-to-face encounter. We should ask what would be most suitable for our family in our situation.

Let us patiently wait for these little beings. Silence and patience — let us apply these guidelines during this time.

In verse 14, the Psalmist proclaims, "I praise You, for I am fearfully and wonderfully made. Wonderful are Your works!" (English Standard Version). Do we have any idea how our bodies will adapt to the life that is developing in them? Everything is falling into place for us to welcome these children. Our bodies are opening up, making room for these beings and preparing to nourish, protect, and preserve them. So let us also praise the Lord for what we are and for the wonder of our bodies.

This can be hard for some people during a period in which we feel nauseated most of the time, have a hard time eating, or experience other difficulties that we have not known until now. We do not feel any of this wonder that is being developed in us; we simply feel sick, tired, and irritated. So, we should surround ourselves with kind people who support us. And let us recall verse 10: "Thy

hand shall lead me, / and thy right hand shall hold me,"
and verses 11 and 12:

> If I say, "Let only darkness cover me,
>     and the light about me be night,"
> even the darkness is not dark to thee,
>     the night is bright as the day;
>     for darkness is as light with thee.

The light will come as certainly as the sun that rises each
morning and even better — in the middle of the night.
Psalm 126 tells us:

> May those who sow in tears
>     reap with shouts of joy!
> He that goes forth weeping,
>     bearing the seed for sowing,
> shall come home with shouts of joy,
>     bringing his sheaves with him. (vv. 5–6)

Therefore, let those who are experiencing difficulties at the
start be confident. Our bag of seeds will bring forth sheaves
that are full, and we will be joyful! Let us lean on the Lord,
who accompanies us no matter what our difficulties are,
and let us not cease to praise Him for this mystery of life
from its start and for the wonders of our bodies.

*For Further Reflection*

We may also meditate on the clay and the master potter who fashions it, allowing ourselves to be permeated by this image (Isa. 45:9–13). The potter takes the time to complete his work. He carefully shapes the clay until it is the way he wants it. Indeed, it is the Lord who models and fashions us as well as our children.

## A Concluding Prayer

*Lord, I praise and thank You for what You are silently doing in me. Thank You for the life of this being You already know, who is being formed. You are the One who, day after day, weaves and fashions him, like a potter who carefully shapes the clay. Thank You also, Lord, for the wonder that I am, for my body and my being. Make me completely open to life and available for Your creative work. Bless this child who is being developed, and may I, every day, be able to bless him in You, His Creator. Amen.*

*Third Month*

# You Are Precious in My Eyes

*But now thus says the LORD,*
*he who created you, O Jacob,*
 *he who formed you, O Israel:*
*"Fear not, for I have redeemed you;*
 *I have called you by name, you are mine.*
*When you pass through the waters I will be with you;*
 *and through the rivers, they shall not overwhelm you;*
*when you walk through fire you shall not be burned,*
 *and the flame shall not consume you.*
*For I am the LORD your God,*
 *the Holy One of Israel, your Savior.*
*I give Egypt as your ransom,*
 *Ethiopia and Seba in exchange for you.*
*Because you are precious in my eyes,*
 *and honored, and I love you,*
*I give men in return for you,*
 *peoples in exchange for your life.*
*Fear not, for I am with you;*
 *I will bring your offspring from the east,*

*and from the west I will gather you;*
*I will say to the north, Give up,*
*and to the south, Do not withhold;*
*bring my sons from afar*
*and my daughters from the end of the earth,*
*every one who is called by my name,*
*whom I created for my glory,*
*whom I formed and made." (Isa. 43:1-7)*

Here we are, once again, facing the Creator God, who formed and fashioned us to manifest His glory. He is also the Creator of our children. Before they belong to us, these new beings belong to God. We are not absolute masters of their lives, and it is good to surrender ourselves to the One who knows these children perfectly.

But God is not a distant Creator who looks at His work from Heaven and congratulates Himself. No, He offers us a special love, a love that is exclusive for each one of us. Let us allow this word to resonate in us, "You are precious in my eyes, and honored, and I love you." Let us be transformed by this immense love of God that is in us and in all His people. We can then glimpse the love the Creator has for these little persons in the making who are being entirely bathed in this communion with the Father. They already belong to Him (Isa. 43:1), just as we belong to Him. Let us be immersed in this word of life that makes us people who are loved and capable of loving.

Many questions can arise in the minds of future mothers: "Will I be capable of loving him? How do I love him as much as his brother or sister?" For certain mothers, the love that is being developed is easy and instantaneous. For others, it is less evident. It grows little by little. Even among siblings, love does not necessarily spring up in the same way. Let us, in all simplicity, repeat this to our children: "You are precious in my eyes, and honored, and I love you."

Saying this word of love to our children can sometimes be difficult for those who have never said "I love you." God can help us. Let us, first of all, allow this word to be activated in our own heart of a child, a woman, and a mother. Let us receive it for ourselves by tirelessly repeating it. God loves us; we are precious in His eyes; and He gives us everything that He has, including His own Son. By dying on the Cross, God gave Himself to the world and to each of us. So, by recalling this love of God for us, perhaps, with the help of the Holy Spirit, these words will arise in us for our children.

We do not yet know what or whom they will resemble, what characteristics they will have, or how they will grow up, but that does not matter. Love does not arise perfectly, but it is full of mercy. God loves us, not in spite of our distractions, our mistakes, or our faults, but even in the midst of these. "For when I am weak, then I am strong," Saint Paul says (2 Cor. 12:10). God wants to dwell with us in our weakness and love us in that very place where we wish to hide. Our children are small and weak and need to be protected and pampered. This is why the Lord has such a special love for them, and we are to love them just the way they are in our wombs today, without worrying ahead of time about how they will be. We are all God's favorite people, just as each of our children, because of his uniqueness, will be our favorite.

Let us end this reflection by meditating on the word that is twice present in this passage, "Fear not" (Isa. 43:1, 5). We also need to repeat it. Let us surrender ourselves to God and chase all fear from our hearts. "When you pass through the waters I will be with you" (v. 2). Going through pregnancy is especially reflected in this text, as much for the baby as for the mother.

But let us not go too fast, and let us calmly deal with this subject during the last months.

May we continue to be certain that the Lord accompanies us on this journey — this passage toward motherhood. He promises not to abandon us; Jerusalem said, "The Lord has forsaken me, my Lord has forgotten me." But the Lord responds, "Can a woman forget her suckling child, that she should have no compassion on the son of her womb? Even these may forget, yet I will not forget you" (Isa. 49:14–15). God is even more faithful than a mother. May we allow ourselves to be loved by this God who is burning with love, and let Him transform our hearts to love our children.

*For Further Reflection*

During this month, we can meditate, once again, on the God of life, who chose us and preferred us and who pours His Spirit upon our children (Isa. 44:1–5). In this passage, the Lord again reminds us not to fear. We can be certain that He accompanies us, He who promises to pour His Spirit on our descendants and His blessing on our offspring (Isa. 44:3). In response to this promise, they will one day say, "I am the LORD's." This must lead and encourage us to pray now for our children that they too will know God's consuming love for them.

## A Concluding Prayer

*Thank You, Lord, for Your infinite love. Thank You for unceasingly telling me that I am precious in Your eyes—You who created me. You chose me to participate in this work of creation. Following Your example, help me know how to say to this child and to my other children how much they are loved and how precious they are. May I always recall that they are, above all, Your children and that they belong to You. Banish all fear from my heart and allow me to become more confident and to love You more. Amen.*

*Fourth Month*

# Jesus and the Little Children

*At that time the disciples came to Jesus and asked, "Who is the greatest in the kingdom of heaven?" He called a child, whom He put among them, and said, "Truly I tell you, unless you change and become like children, you will never enter the kingdom of heaven. Whoever becomes humble like this child is the greatest in the kingdom of heaven. Whoever receives one such child in my name receives me. (Matt. 18: 1–5)*

In this passage, Jesus exhorts us to become like children, which is required to enter the Kingdom. So, to be great, it is necessary to become little and to humble oneself. It is a paradox: Can we become children again once we are adults? This is the question that Nicodemus will ask Jesus, "Can a man enter a second time into his mother's womb and be born?" (see John 3:4). But in both cases, in the passage above and to Nicodemus, Jesus is talking about the need to be born again in order to be able to see the Kingdom of God.

To understand this teaching, let us contemplate a newborn in the arms of his parent. He survives only through his parents and thanks to them. If he had been separated from his mother before the pregnancy normally ended, his life would have been imperiled. In the womb, he was nourished, thanks to his mother, and because of the exchange between the two of them, he grew, cradled in amniotic fluid. When he was born, he could not have lived on his own. In order to develop, he needs others to take care of him, to feed him, to change him, to protect him from the cold, and to caress him. It is mandatory that the person taking care of him be attentive to his needs, be they physical or emotional.

This image can remind us of how God cradles us and consoles us and gives us what we need every day. When we consent to have God as our Father and to be His children, depending on Him for everything, we are like newborns. It is He who makes us live. He takes care of us and waits for us to hand our lives over to Him. What can we do by ourselves? Nothing; He gives us the grace.

As our babies grow in us, let us humble ourselves and become like them. They receive everything from their mothers to survive. Let us also be dependent on the Lord and allow Him to nourish us, cradle us, and make us grow.

"Whoever receives one such child in my name receives me" (Matt. 18:5). Are we aware of the power of this verse — that it is really the same thing to receive a baby as to receive Jesus Himself? In this way, we can experience the holy presence of the Savior in our wombs. Fully receiving and welcoming our children is the same as fully receiving and welcoming Jesus the Lord. It is an extraordinary mystery.

A woman once told me that she took care of her baby as if he were Jesus. How right she was! By welcoming the baby in us, may we be aware of the holiness of his presence and of Jesus in him. Let us welcome him as if he were our Savior Jesus Christ; let us take very good care of this being who is in us today.

Some could object that I am already making this child a king. In a certain sense, this is true! But he is not a king who does everything he wants to do in a tyrannical way. No, he is a humble little king, who sometimes suffers and is able to cry, shout, and call for help.

Jesus is not an overbearing king. He makes Himself a servant. He took on flesh in the body of a woman; He was a vulnerable little being. So, let us welcome our children like this poor, humble, suffering Jesus, who lifts His face toward us, and let us imagine our bodies as tabernacles to receive Him.

Starting now, we can also entrust to the Lord the god-parents we will choose; they will receive these children through the love of Jesus and will be charged with raising them in Jesus with us. Let us pray to be enlightened to choose people who will know how to be present for our children in moments of joy, doubt, and difficulties, and who will be able to help them to know Jesus.

This choice is sometimes difficult. We can feel obligated to ask a certain person in the family, or we might have no one left to ask after many births. Nonetheless, let us be aware that this choice is important for our children and pray that our decisions will be enlightened by the Holy Spirit.

*For Further Reflection*

During this month, let us also meditate on the Last Judgment and the welcoming of the just into the Kingdom:

> I was hungry and you gave me food, I was thirsty and you gave me drink, I was a stranger and you welcomed me, I was naked and you clothed me, I was sick and you visited me, I was in prison and you came to me.... Truly, I say to you, as you did it to one of the least of these my brethren, you did it to me. (Matt. 25:35–40)

Let us take care of these weak, vulnerable beings, who are our babies, and whom we feed, clothe, and welcome when they are born, as if they were Jesus Himself in our ordinary daily lives.

## A Concluding Prayer

*Father, thank You for Your Word. Thank You for showing us Your respect and love for the littlest ones. To receive them is to receive Jesus. May I be able to welcome this life in me, as if it were You in person who came to take flesh in me. Lord, place Your hands on this child and bless him. May I be able to take care of him without ever forgetting Your holy presence in him. Inspire us to choose godparents in accordance with Your heart. Amen.*

*Fifth Month*

# The Visitation

*In those days Mary arose and went with haste into the hill country, to a city of Judah, and she entered the house of Zechariah and greeted Elizabeth. And when Elizabeth heard the greeting of Mary, the babe leaped in her womb; and Elizabeth was filled with the Holy Spirit and she exclaimed with a loud cry, "Blessed are you among women, and blessed is the fruit of your womb! And why is this granted me, that the mother of my Lord should come to me? For behold, when the voice of your greeting came to my ears, the babe in my womb leaped for joy. And blessed is she who believed that there would be a fulfilment of what was spoken to her from the Lord." And Mary said,*

> *"My soul magnifies the Lord,*
> *and my spirit rejoices in God my Savior,*
> *for he has regarded the low estate of his*
>     *handmaiden.*
> *For behold, henceforth all generations will*
> *call me blessed;*

*for he who is mighty has done great things*
    *for me,*
*and holy is his name.*
*And his mercy is on those who fear him*
*from generation to generation.*
*He has shown strength with his arm,*
*he has scattered the proud in the imagination*
*of their hearts,*
*he has put down the mighty from their*
    *thrones,*
*and exalted those of low degree;*
*he has filled the hungry with good things,*
*and the rich he has sent empty away.*
*He has helped his servant Israel,*
*in remembrance of his mercy,*
*as he spoke to our fathers,*
*to Abraham and to his posterity for ever."*
    *And Mary remained with her about three months,*
*and returned to her home. (Luke 1:39–56)*

After the angel's announcement, Mary went to the home of her cousin Elizabeth, who had been pregnant for about six months. Let us imagine the meeting of these two women. As we start to feel the movements of the babies in us, let us linger over these words: "When Elizabeth heard the greeting of Mary, the babe leaped in her womb." Elizabeth was filled with the Holy Spirit and cried out in a loud voice, "Blessed are you among women, and blessed is the fruit of your womb! And why is this granted me, that the mother of my Lord should come to me? For behold, when the voice of your greeting came to my ears, the babe in my womb leaped for joy." Elizabeth's baby, from inside her, noticed that something was going on and "leaped for joy." He was hidden and protected from the outside world but was already connected to it.

Our babies experience important events; they move and react to what is going on around them, particularly when their fathers, mothers, and siblings take the time to communicate with him. They curl up against the hand that gently presses against them from outside the womb; in this way, they set up an unusual contact between the outside and the inside worlds.

Elizabeth's child felt that there was something important going on in Mary's womb, and this encounter caused him to leap with joy. He, and his mother through him, understood that the child whom Mary bore was not an ordinary being. Elizabeth, who was filled with the Holy Spirit, noticed, through the movement of her child, that Mary was the mother of her Savior, though Jesus had hardly begun to develop! This is extraordinary. If John leaped with joy and felt the presence of Jesus in his mother's womb, the babies whom we carry can also be sensitive to the Savior's presence. Let us speak to them about Jesus now, and sing psalms and canticles to them, and repeat that the Lord loves them. The closer we are to Jesus, the more our babies will leap for joy at the mention of His name!

Let us therefore be attentive to the movements of the hidden little beings we are carrying, who are already fully present. We are not to feel guilty when we go through moments of sadness, anger, or strong misunderstandings with others. At such times, we might ask ourselves, "What am I causing my baby to experience?" But our emotions, even the negative ones, are an integral part of our lives, and it would be impossible to cut ourselves off from them or to bury them without ever expressing them. Emotions in themselves are neither good nor bad, but we are responsible for what we do with them.

The shifting of emotions is completely normal in a pregnancy, during which we can go from feeling happy to feeling very discouraged within a few seconds. This is sometimes very disconcerting for our families! Let us not worry about it, but let us be attentive to what we are experiencing and know how to put everything into the Father's hands. May we talk to our children with simplicity about the emotions we are experiencing and find places to discharge them—to a friendly, attentive ear and in prayer. By accompanying the life we are carrying to the end, may we also choose to go toward life and toward that which gives us life.

Finally, we can dwell on Mary's canticle (Luke 1:46–55). With the help of the Holy Spirit and like Mary, we can compose a canticle for our children, praising and thanking the Lord for all the marvels He does for us. May we repeat it (or sing it!) day after day. In the Hebrew tradition, a canticle for a newborn child is often composed. Following Mary's example, we can point out to our children what we are experiencing through prayer and praising during this pregnancy. It is a time when our emotional hypersensitivity can also be spiritual in nature. The canticle we will compose will be strongly marked by all that we will have experienced with the Lord and with our children during these months.

## For Further Reflection

To perfect our meditation about what we are going through, we can be attentive to our interior motions, these movements within us that impel us to feel consoled or desolate. These are, in fact, reflections of our interior life that push us toward joy that lasts or toward desolation. They are especially developed by Saint Ignatius of Loyola. Saint Paul exhorts us to allow ourselves to be led by the Holy Spirit: "If we live by the Spirit, let us also walk by the Spirit" (Gal. 5:25). The fruits of the Spirit that are cited—love, joy, peace, patience, kindness, goodness, faithfulness, gentleness, and self-control—are great consolations for our souls. Through them, we experience zeal and spiritual desire. Our hearts open up. On the contrary, desolation causes us to be sad, anguished, and discouraged; we ask ourselves what the point is. Certain great witnesses or saints talk about the "dark night of the soul," which has sometimes lasted for several years (in Saint Thérèse of Lisieux, for example). When we feel desolate, let us recall the consolations we have received (hence, the importance of noting them!) and seek to ground ourselves in our reality without being too emotionally upset about what is happening to us. May we search for what produces fruit in our lives by allowing the Holy Spirit to operate more often in us.

## A Concluding Prayer

*Lord, who provoked so much joy in John, a little child still in the womb of his mother, Elizabeth, give me Your joy as I feel my baby move in me. May these movements be a dance of love for me, leading us toward You. Help me to respect him as a being who is worthy and unique, in order for him to feel secure. And if I, at times, feel anxious or discouraged, Lord, help me simply to surrender myself to You and fearlessly and lovingly speak to my baby. May the Holy Spirit inspire me to sing holy canticles to praise Your name and the wonders that You accomplish in me, and may I be able to proclaim them every day! Amen.*

# The Revelation of the Name

*Now the time came for Elizabeth to be delivered, and she gave birth to a son. And her neighbors and kinsfolk heard that the Lord had shown great mercy to her, and they rejoiced with her. And on the eighth day they came to circumcise the child; and they would have named him Zechariah after his father, but his mother said, "Not so; he shall be called John." And they said to her, "None of your kindred is called by this name." And they made signs to his father, inquiring what he would have him called. And he asked for a writing tablet, and wrote, "His name is John." And they all marveled. And immediately his mouth was opened and his tongue loosed, and he spoke, blessing God. And fear came on all their neighbors. And all these things were talked about through all the hill country of Judea; and all who heard them laid them up in their hearts, saying, "What then will this child be?" For the hand of the Lord was with him. (Luke 1:57–66)*

This text invites us to meditate on the name that was given to the infant. "His name is John," Zechariah says. Giving a child a name is not easily done. It can be difficult to get others to agree on it! It is even worse if we need to choose two names in the case of twins or if the sex is unknown. There is no way out!

The aim of this meditation is to stress the importance of this choice that the child must take on for his whole life. In the Bible, when God calls people, He very often gives them a new name. For example, Jesus gives Simon the name Peter: "You are Peter, and on this rock I will build my church" (Matt. 16:18). Thus, Jesus shows him his vocation, the role he is to play in the budding Church, as well as the solidity of this Church. We can also cite Abraham, who was called Abram at first: "No longer shall your name be Abram, but your name shall be Abraham; for I have made you the father of a multitude of nations" (Gen. 17:5). Likewise, "As for Sarai your wife, you shall not call her name Sarai, but Sarah shall be her name. I will bless her, and moreover I will give you a son by her" (Gen. 17:15–16).

When monks enter orders, they also receive new names. It is like a new birth for them. A new name, therefore, is not insignificant. In certain cultures, it is customary to wait until the child's personality is revealed to give him a name that will truly fit him. In this passage from St. Luke, we see that the choice of the name John goes against the cultural habits of the era, when the chosen name was that of the father or someone in the family. In our culture, not so long ago, the tradition was the same. Those who do genealogical research will see that it was not rare to give the same name over many generations. And if someone came up with a name that was somewhat original, he had to prove to the registrar of births, marriages, and deaths that this name already existed.

Nowadays, we see the opposite tendency. We can give whatever names we want to our children and even invent names if that pleases us. The name chosen really has to impact the child negatively in order for the registrar of births, marriages, and deaths to oppose it.

But have we thought of the impact of the name on a child and of what we tell him by giving him that name? A name is really a gift that we give this being who is coming into the world. Therefore, it is important to make it meaningful.

We see in the text how the name John is revealed to his parents, and that they affirm it in front of everyone and against all expectations. From this moment on, Zechariah speaks again, and it is not insignificant that God chooses precisely this moment. The man gives a name and is able to talk again. Zechariah enters into God's plan for his son, who will become the one who prepares the way of the Lord.

In the beginning, God created with His word, "God said ..." and it came to pass. Then He gave man the power to name the things that He created: "The man gave names to all cattle, and to the birds of the air, and to every beast of the field" (Gen. 2:20). Thus, Adam named everything that exists on the earth, including the woman: "This at last is bone of my bones and flesh of my flesh, she shall be called Woman" (Gen. 2:23).

The name makes things and beings exist for themselves; it gives them their meaning, and no name is randomly chosen. We see that man names things and beings in the Bible. Thus, God says to Joseph, "You shall call His name Jesus" (Matt. 1:21). Likewise, Zechariah is asked to confirm the name John, which his wife had announced. In Scripture, we see that naming is a paternal grace.

So, even if the name is chosen by both spouses, we can say that the man, by looking at what is special in his child, recognizes him as a special being and "births" him. Therefore, the presence of the father is more than necessary for the growth of the child, who grows while his mother and father are watching him.

So let us pray to find a good name. May we give it time, hand over this choice to the Lord, and ask His Holy Spirit to enlighten us. Let us share our ideas as a couple. This name must resonate in us in a very special way, and it is beautiful to explain to a child why we have chosen this name for him rather than another one, even if the reason is very simple. It is already a sign of the attention that we are showing this child.

*For Further Reflection*

We can also pray with the passage from Revelation that tells us that only in Heaven will we recognize our true name, which is given by God Himself: "I will give him a white stone, with a new name written on the stone which no one knows except him who receives it" (Rev. 2:17). This will be a unique name, which is suitable for everyone, and we will be able to say that this name is the mark of God in us — a marvelous, luminous name that will reveal us as God sees us.

## A Concluding Prayer

*Holy Spirit, the living breath of God, we entrust to You the name that we will give our child at his birth. May it be inspired by You, and may our child rejoice at the sound of his name! Blessed are You, Jesus, for calling us by our name and for knowing each of us intimately. You called Mary Magdalene, a witness of Your Resurrection, by her name, and at that moment she recognized You. May we also hear You call each of us by our name and respond to Your call. Amen.*

*Seventh Month*

# The Storm That Was Calmed

*And when he got into the boat, his disciples followed him. And behold, there arose a great storm on the sea, so that the boat was being swamped by the waves; but he was asleep. And they went and woke him, saying, "Save, Lord; we are perishing." And he said to them, "Why are you afraid, O men of little faith?" Then he rose and rebuked the winds and the sea; and there was a great calm. And the men marveled, saying, "What sort of man is this, that even winds and sea obey him?" (Matt. 8:23–27)*

Here we are in the midst of the birth preparation. This moment can scare us and seem to be an insurmountable test when we think of this verse: "I will greatly multiply your pain in childbearing; in pain you shall bring forth children" (Gen. 3:16). This consequence of sin cripples and frightens us.

Before continuing with this reflection, let us look at Matthew's text, where the sea, which was calm before, lashes out like a true storm. Nothing seems to be able to calm it. The image of the waters being unleashed mirrors childbirth well—the loss of water, the impression of no longer having control and of being carried by a current that is too strong to fight against.

We must prepare for that. Childbirth is a fundamental moment in a woman's life; it remains forever etched in her memory. We see how women love to talk to each other about every detail of their childbirth! Even if it cannot be experienced in an ideal way and is unique for everyone, we can prepare ourselves for the storm that will lead us to encounter our children, whatever the childbirth may be like. In fact, the baby who comes out of the womb cannot avoid provoking this storm, even if the birth takes place in the best conditions. Our whole body participates in this birth. It is waiting for what will happen. It is moving.

The Scripture passage tells us that Jesus is sleeping. Let us contemplate the scene for a moment. The disciples are very scared, and the boat is covered by waves. We hear their cry: "Lord, save us! We are perishing!" We see their despair. We imagine the waves that submerge the boat, the sound of the wind, and the sea that moans and is agitated. How is one not to give in to panic? Death is near. Jesus is sleeping. Would we not feel like shaking Him? "Where are You, Lord? I am being carried away, and You are sleeping? Wake up!" The disciples shout at Jesus. The water is rising.

Let us now observe the attitude of Jesus, once He is awakened by the disciples. He asks them, "Why are you afraid?" He speaks severely to the water and the winds, and everything is calm again. Thus, the disciples are astonished. How is that possible?

This text has many things to tell us about Jesus, and the parallel with our subject can seem a little hasty. Nonetheless, we can so easily put ourselves in the scared disciples' place and hear what Jesus says that makes us doubt. Where is our faith? Can Jesus not calm everything down in an instant? Why do we not trust Him more?

Suffering is a great mystery that sometimes leaves us feeling powerless. Like the disciples, we could say, "Where were You, Lord, when I was suffering? You were sleeping." Nonetheless, Jesus is in the boat. He also endures the storm, the waves, and the wind. His attitude is different; He is peaceful; He is sleeping, for He is not afraid. He is calm in the midst of the unleashing of the elements.

We can learn from this attitude. We sometimes struggle in our trials and feel like giving up. May we not be afraid to be in the boat; our Savior accompanies us. Let us not be afraid of the storm that is unleashing with more or less energy in this event of our lives—the accompaniment of a child during his birth; Jesus is there.

Let us allow ourselves to be in His arms, to surrender, and to let the contraction that comes like a wave go by, and may we contemplate it from afar. It arrives and splashes us, but it does not carry us away. May we not try to go against it—it could knock us over and sink us—but let us accompany it in its movement. We are with it and follow it, and through these wave-contractions, our little ones come, descend, and also cross this long, sometimes tumultuous tunnel to encounter us. Jesus will be there to welcome them and see them being born.

In this regard, the Japanese painter Katsushika Hokusai's famous painting called *The Great Wave off Kanagawa* is especially revealing, as is his *Cascade of Amida*, which makes one think of the loss of water. In contemplating these paintings, we cannot help but rejoice in the beauty of the birth of a child.

We do not come out of pregnancy unchanged. We are the same woman and, at the same time, different. These children make us become mothers and lead us in a dance that is new and unknown every time. Suffering takes on another meaning without our seeking it; it is not against us; it is with us and, somewhere, it brings us into the world.

*For Further Reflection*

Let us especially meditate on this passage: "We know that the whole creation has been groaning in labor pains until now" (see Rom. 8:22).

Paul shows us how all creation is waiting with eager longing for the promised deliverance — namely, life eternal (Rom. 8:18–27). Like a baby, who goes from his mother's womb to the outside world, we can certainly believe that we will go from this world to the heavenly world for which we were made. There is a deliverance for the child as well as for his mother. The baby also experiences childbirth as an earthquake. Nonetheless, this passage is necessary for life. This unique encounter is the one that makes us live and wait throughout these long months. In this way, we can understand waiting to meet the Lord, when we will be able to see Him face-to-face.

## A Concluding Prayer

*Jesus, You who knew suffering and who went through it in order to have all men come to You, I now hand over to You the moment of my childbirth. Help me to know how to accompany my child as he is being born; help me to open myself to allow him to pass through me. Accompany me all throughout this work of childbirth; may it help me to give birth to life. May I go forth in confidence and faith even when the storm will be strong, knowing that You are with me and that You will never abandon me. Let this meeting with my baby be truly a meeting of love, and may You also be present in this meeting. Amen.*

*Eighth Month*

# The Nativity

*In those days a decree went out from Caesar Augustus that all the world should be enrolled. This was the first enrollment, when Quirinius was governor of Syria. And all went to be enrolled, each to his own city. And Joseph also went up from Galilee, from the city of Nazareth, to Judea, to the city of David, which is called Bethlehem, because he was of the house and lineage of David, to be enrolled with Mary, his betrothed, who was with child. And while they were there, the time came for her to be delivered. And she gave birth to her first-born son and wrapped him in swaddling cloths, and laid him in a manger, because there was no place for them in the inn.*

*And in that region there were shepherds out in the field, keeping watch over their flock by night. And an angel of the Lord appeared to them, and the glory of the Lord shone around them, and they were filled with fear. And the angel said to them, "Be not afraid; for behold, I bring you good news of a great joy which will come to all the people; for to you is born this day in the city of David a Savior, who is Christ the Lord. And this will be a sign for you: you will find a babe wrapped in swaddling cloths and lying in a manger." And suddenly there was with the angel a multitude of the heavenly host praising God and saying,*

    *"Glory to God in the highest,*
    *and on earth peace among men with whom*
    *he is pleased!"*

    *When the angels went away from them into heaven, the shepherds said to one another, "Let us go over to Bethlehem and see this thing that has happened, which the Lord has made known to us." And they went with haste, and found Mary and Joseph, and the babe lying in a manger. And when they saw it they made known the saying which had been told them concerning this child; and all who heard it wondered at what the shepherds told them. But Mary kept all these things, pondering them in her heart. And the shepherds returned, glorifying and praising God for all they had heard and seen, as it had been told them. (Luke 2:1–20)*

The time of birth has not yet quite arrived, but we can now start to meditate on Jesus' Nativity.

When we immerse ourselves in the verses that speak of Christ's birth, we become very calm. This calm, nevertheless, is not connected to the events that could, on the contrary, justifiably agitate us — that there is no room for the Holy Family in the dwellings that are usually anticipated for travelers. Mary is forced to give birth in a stable. Let us imagine what it would be like for us to give birth in such conditions!

Let us observe Mary's emptying of herself and this baby, the Savior of the world, in this manger. Jesus, sleeping in a manger, will become the Bread of Life, this Bread that we consume each Sunday. God's plan is perfectly fulfilled; nothing is left to chance; the prophecies are accomplished, and the events become meaningful.

Where does the calm that comes from this account originate? We can ask ourselves this question: Where are the things we need? These days, we must absolutely have everything prepared and must stick to the careful preparations we have made for the birth. It is also crucial to have found the most reliable hospital, to have rewall-papered the bedroom, to have packed everything on the list given to us by the hospital. In short, we have to be completely ready.

Of course, my aim is not to say we must not prepare, for the welcoming of a newborn also entails this material preparation and the effort one puts into it, and it is important to choose what is suitable for our children. But if all this material preparation is necessary, it could be that the most important thing is not in it. A divine peace comes from the manger, this simple place that is not pleasing. Whatever the situations in our lives may be, including our childbirth, let us be receptive to this peace, which does not depend so much on outer appearances as it does on our interior life. It relies not on acting but on being. Thus, while taking care of what needs to be done, let us not forget to *be* first, by searching for peace and simplicity. For it is there that we will encounter real joy. May we look for what is conducive to the interior life and our relationships and organize our daily lives accordingly. In this way, prayer is no longer an option; it becomes essential to prepare us to welcome these children.

Let us now look at the faces of the shepherds, who are the first to be told of Christ's birth. These poor people are very scared. Are we not filled with fear? Questions and worries sometimes agitate us. Are we ready to welcome a baby? Will we know how to take care of him? Is there anything we have forgotten? The angels say, "Do not be afraid." How I love to repeat these words. The angels praise God and tell us that God "gives peace to the men He loves." Let Him love us, look at us, and love and look at our babies. And may Heaven be completely joyful with us!

Like Mary, let us keep these events in our hearts and not forget them. May we be able to review and remember the moment of our children's births, that time when, by emptying ourselves, we accept our no longer being in control of the situation. We must surrender and accept the "cradle," the area of our poverty and powerlessness. In fact, it is difficult to accept that we cannot master everything and that everything is not perfect, as we had foreseen at the start. We want to look happy, to show others that everything is going well, and we do not dare reveal ourselves as we are, with our weaknesses.

The birth of a child exposes us, in the literal as well as the figurative sense of the word. We do not give birth with our clothes on, right? Likewise, we must remove all the skins that we have put on to protect ourselves, like armor. Jesus, through the manger, shows us His love for little children, for those who know they are poor and feeble. It is in this hidden place in us that He wants to reveal Himself. "Those who are well have no need of a physician, but those who are sick," He will say (Matt. 9:12). And Saint Paul will dare say, "When I am weak, then I am strong" (2 Cor. 12:10).

As soon as we, like Joseph, Mary, and Jesus, agree to empty ourselves and discover where our poverty lies, what grace we will receive! Jesus comes to live in us, and we can show ourselves as we are. Then, like the shepherds who also live very simply, we can hear the song of the angels, who praise the glory of God. As soon as our children are born, let us rejoice with them! New life is starting on the earth!

*For Further Reflection*

To perfect our meditations, we can read and pray with this passage about Martha and Mary: "Martha, Martha, you are anxious and troubled about many things; one thing is needful. Mary has chosen the good portion, which shall not be taken away from her" (Luke 10:41–42). In these last preparations, we often get agitated. Let us not forget what is most important and what will allow us to encounter our children in the truest, most profound way. Let us take time to listen to Jesus' word and allow it to nourish us. May we not hesitate to put it on our calendars so that we will be sure to make it a regular part of our day.

## A Concluding Prayer

*Gentle Jesus, little Child who is sleeping in a manger, You who nourish me day after day, help me to empty myself of all affectation. May I know that the best part is dwelling near You. Calm my agitation and fears. May the peace You want to give me reach my heart, which is the place of the greatest chaos! And may I, with the angels, be able to praise and sing Your Name, You, the God of the humble, little ones. Amen.*

*Ninth Month*

# The Welcoming of the Child

*O LORD, my heart is not lifted up,*
  *my eyes are not raised too high;*
*I do not occupy myself with things*
  *too great and too marvelous for me.*
*But I have calmed and quieted my soul,*
  *like a child quieted at its mother's breast;*
  *like a child that is quieted is my soul.*
  *O Israel, hope in the LORD*
  *from this time forth and for evermore.*
  *(Ps. 131)*

*Before she was in labor*
  *she gave birth;*
*before her pain came upon her*
  *she was delivered of a son.*
*Who has heard such a thing?*
  *Who has seen such things?*
*Shall a land be born in one day?*

*Shall a nation be brought forth*
     *in one moment?*
*For as soon as Zion was in labor*
     *she brought forth her sons.*
*Shall I bring to the birth and not cause to bring forth?*
     *says the LORD;*
*shall I, who cause to bring forth, shut the womb?*
     *says your God.*
*"Rejoice with Jerusalem, and be glad for her,*
     *all you who love her;*
*rejoice with her in joy,*
     *all you who mourn over her;*
*that you may suck and be satisfied*
     *with her consoling breasts;*
*that you may drink deeply with delight*
     *from the abundance of her glory."*
*For thus says the LORD:*
*"Behold, I will extend prosperity to her like a river,*
     *and the wealth of the nations like an overflowing*
     *stream;*
*and you shall suck, you shall be carried upon her hip,*
     *and dandled upon her knees.*
*As one whom his mother comforts,*
     *so I will comfort you;*
     *you shall be comforted in Jerusalem.*

## The Welcoming of the Child

*You shall see, and your heart shall rejoice;*
  *your bones shall flourish like the grass;*
*and it shall be known that the hand of the LORD is*
*with his servants,*
  *and his indignation is against his enemies."*
  *(Isa. 66:7–14)*

B ut I have calmed and quieted my soul, / like a child quieted at its mother's breast; / like a child that is quieted is my soul." The child is calm and peaceful near his mother. We are called to adopt this attitude of confidence and surrender toward our Father.

A baby curled up in the womb has started his existence for himself, and nonetheless, he is completely bonded with his mother. He does not yet know he is a different person from his mother. We say that a newborn baby cannot do anything by himself, yet he is very competent. He knows how to cry when he needs something, and his body speaks for him when he is bothered or relaxed. In someone's arms, he fearlessly falls asleep. He can also cry in the same arms that comfort him; he knows that there, he has an attentive ear that listens to him and that will best respond to his needs, whether physiological or emotional.

The newborn's calm and confident attitude often co-exists with the agitation that hovers over a birth. The medical team comes and goes, and, in the hospital or at home, family and friends want to surround us, to see the baby, and to offer gifts. So, it is important to know how to preserve this unique moment of birth. This newborn child is worthy of a thoughtful, calm, peaceful welcome. Mother and child need to get to know each other. Let us insist, especially with the medical personnel, that these first moments not be stolen from us and that they be intimate if our care or our children's care is not urgent. And if it is not possible (in the case of a Caesarian section or a premature birth, for example), let us try to re-create these first moments as soon as we can. We can engage in skin-to-skin contact, for example, after a relatively smooth birth in a peaceful, intimate setting that includes the father — just the three of us.

May we calmly welcome these babies; let us stop being agitated after the turbulence of the childbirth, contemplate our newborn children, and take the time to welcome them. Let us stay calm, and may this peace enlighten us about the surrender of our lives into the Lord's hands.

In Isaiah's text, the image of a mother who takes care of her child shows how the Lord will take care of His people. Let us see this mother who has just given birth and feeds her baby, who is carried on her hip, cuddled on her knees, and consoled. This is how the Lord wants to take care of us!

God, the merciful Father, as we often call Him, also has the womb of a mother. The word "mercy" comes from the word "uterus" in Hebrew. The link between the two words is very strong, and the comparison is quite old. God turns toward His children, consoles them, and carries them in Himself.

Let us take care of our babies as the Lord takes care of His people. May we see the joy and contentment of a baby who is fed and the peace of a baby who is carried and cuddled. May we silence the little voice (or big voice!) in us that would say to us, "You are going to spoil this child." Are we not the spoiled children of the Father? He does not hesitate to console and carry us on His knees when we are only infants who are still sucking the milk of His word. So, may we take the time to be with our babies and learn to get to know each other. Everything is not necessarily immediately simple.

"You shall see, and your heart shall rejoice; / your bones shall flourish like the grass; / and it shall be known that the hand of the LORD is with his servants" (Isa. 66:14). The weariness of childbirth and of the nine months of pregnancy can still be great, and yet, do we not feel ourselves coming alive and filled with love and joy with a baby in our arms? We can hang on to this beautiful promise when we feel sad after the birth—when we are experiencing baby blues. Our bodies and hearts are made for life—to come back to life! What a revealing and marvelous image of the work that God wants to accomplish in us!

"Shall I bring to the birth and not cause to bring forth? / says the LORD; / shall I, who cause to bring forth, shut the womb? / says your God" (Isa. 66:9). May this verse accompany us to the end of these nine months and help us to be filled with confidence in facing the event for which we are preparing.

*For Further Reflection*

The Song of Songs is often quoted to show the love of a husband and wife and, by analogy, of God and His Church. Thus, we and our husbands can often read it as a couple to stay firmly united in order to experience this great event that is going to change our lives. Our family is going to grow, and each member will have to find his place again. May our love, which is a priority, be always stronger and, despite the unavoidable tasks that are connected to the care of a baby in the home, let us also take care of our beloved and rejoice in his presence beside us.

"The voice of my beloved! Behold, he comes, leaping upon the mountains, bounding over the hills" (Song of Sol. 2:8).

## A Concluding Prayer

*Good Father, who is full of mercy for Your children, You give us the joy of welcoming a baby in our home. May we be able to be attentive to his reception in our world, and may his arrival be filled with respect and love, in a calm and thoughtful atmosphere. Make us loving parents, in Your image, who know how to surrender into Your tender, fatherly arms. Amen.*

*As the father of this child who is going to be born, may I be able to sustain and help the one You gave me for a wife during the time of the birth. May I know how to accompany her with all the love that I give her, and let me stay close to her side. Help me to welcome this child, whom I am going to discover for the first time, and to love him with the heart of a father, who is turned toward You.*

# The Presentation of Jesus in the Temple

And at the end of eight days, when he was circumcised, he was called Jesus, the name given by the angel before he was conceived in the womb.

And when the time came for their purification according to the law of Moses, they brought him up to Jerusalem to present him to the Lord (as it is written in the law of the Lord, "Every male that opens the womb shall be called holy to the Lord") and to offer a sacrifice according to what is said in the law of the Lord, "a pair of turtledoves, or two young pigeons." Now there was a man in Jerusalem, whose name was Simeon, and this man was righteous and devout, looking for the consolation of Israel, and the Holy Spirit was upon him. And it had been revealed to him by the Holy Spirit that he should not see death before he had seen the Lord's Christ. And inspired by the Spirit he came into the temple; and when the parents brought in the child Jesus, to do for him according to the custom of the law, he took him up in his arms and blessed God and said,

*"Lord, now lettest thou thy servant depart in*
    *peace,*
*according to thy word;*
*for mine eyes have seen thy salvation*
*which thou hast prepared in the presence of all*
    *peoples,*
*a light for revelation to the Gentiles,*
*and for glory to thy people Israel."*

*And his father and his mother marveled at what was said about him; and Simeon blessed them and said to Mary his mother,*

*"Behold, this child is set for the fall and rising of*
*many in Israel,*
*and for a sign that is spoken against*
*(and a sword will pierce through your own soul*
    *also),*
*that thoughts out of many hearts may be revealed."*

*And there was a prophetess, Anna, the daughter of Phanuel, of the tribe of Asher; she was of a great age, having lived with her husband seven years from her virginity, and as a widow till she was eighty-four. She did not depart from the temple, worshiping with fasting and prayer night and day. And coming up at that very hour she gave thanks to God, and spoke of him to all who were looking for the redemption of Jerusalem.*

*And when they had performed everything according to the law of the Lord, they returned into Galilee, to their own city, Nazareth. And the child grew and became strong, filled with wisdom; and the favor of God was upon him. (Luke 2:21–40)*

In the Hebrew tradition, the eighth day was the day of the child's circumcision and the day when the father gave a name to the child. Later, the ritual purification of the mother was on the fourth day after the birth. The child was also presented to God for Him to bless the child.

There is something very beautiful in this Jewish custom; from the time of his birth, the child is presented to God. He is entrusted to Him, in the presence of his parents and in front of the assembly. In the passage from Luke, Simeon and Anna, who are impelled by the Holy Spirit, prophesy and bless the child and His mother and father.

We talked earlier about our meditations, recalling the canticles of Mary and Zechariah, and about writing a prayer and a canticle of praise to the Lord for our children a few days after their birth. Let us not hesitate to do it when our baby is born and to bless the Lord for His presence among us. What a welcoming gift!

This prayer can be presented to the Lord with the child on the eighth day. It will result in very simply reuniting the close family members of the child (parents and possibly the godfather and godmother) who will be helping to educate him in the Faith. We can also include his brothers and sisters, who will be welcoming a new arrival in the family as well and who sometimes have very mixed feelings toward him. This prayer (which is not at all required) can be a spiritual offering. It lets us face the infinite goodness of God, who entrusts us with these children, and our littleness before what remains to be accomplished.

We do not need to turn this moment into a big family feast—rest must be a priority for the young parents, who are still very tired—but it is essential to take the time to pray a simple prayer to entrust our children to the Lord. Let us bless Him together for the gift He gives us of this new life in our hands.

If it has not already been done, let us also pray to find godparents who will know how to help our children grow in the Lord. May we listen to the words they will be able to give us for the baby, like Anna and Simeon, who received prophetic words for Jesus and His parents. These words can accompany not only our children but also us parents.

"Simeon blessed them." He blessed Mary and Joseph and not only Jesus in their arms. As parents, we also need to receive words of encouragement and blessing, which remind us that we are not alone in raising our children. Simeon was guided by the Spirit. The Holy Spirit urged him to go to the Temple and look at the Newborn, and He inspired him to say words of blessing and prophecies. Simeon had confidence in God's promise to him that he would not die before having seen the Savior. We are told, "His father and his mother marveled at what was said about him." They did not immediately understand what was being said to them. So, let us confidently and simply receive the words that will be given to us. Like Mary, may we keep them in our hearts, like a treasure.

The Jewish tradition is that a prayer of blessing is presented in each of the day's actions (upon rising, going to bed, during meals, while working, washing one's hands, or any other event). A rabbi said that each man must say one hundred blessings a day.

So, may we call down God's blessing on our children and recall that we are not alone, and let us be accompanied by God's Word. This reception that we reserve for them through a prayer of praise and blessing gives them their unique place as children not only in our hearts but also in God's.

*For Further Reflection*

We can let ourselves be permeated by the canticle of Zechariah (Luke 1:67–79), who prophesied, being filled with the Holy Spirit after the birth of his son, John. This canticle, which is sung every day in the Church's morning Office, can also inspire us to praise God for our newborn children and help us to find the words to thank Him for what He is doing for us.

## A Concluding Prayer

*My whole being blesses the Lord! May Your Holy Name be praised, Lord, for You have given us the precious gift of a new life. May Your blessing rest on this child. Fill his spirit with wisdom, love, and mercy; may he serve You all the days of his life and learn to know Your great love for him. May You be praised for the confidence and surrender of this little being who is in our arms; may Your holy angels praise You and all men with them! Lord, You perform such great marvels! Amen.*

# The Role of Women and Mothers

*But Mary stood weeping outside the tomb, and as she wept she stooped to look into the tomb; and she saw two angels in white, sitting where the body of Jesus had lain, one at the head and one at the feet. They said to her, "Woman, why are you weeping?" She said to them, "Because they have taken away my Lord, and I do not know where they have laid him."*

*Saying this, she turned round and saw Jesus standing, but she did not know that it was Jesus. Jesus said to her, "Woman, why are you weeping? Whom do you seek?" Supposing him to be the gardener, she said to him, "Sir, if you have carried him away, tell me where you have laid him, and I will take him away." Jesus said to her, "Mary." She turned and said to him in Hebrew, "Rabboni!" (which means Teacher). Jesus said to her, "Do not hold me, for I have not yet ascended to the Father; but go to my brethren and say to them, I am ascending to my Father and your Father, to my God and your God." Mary Magdalene*

*went and said to the disciples, "I have seen the Lord";
and she told them that he had said these things to her.
(John 20:11–18)*

In this passage from the Gospel of John, Mary Magdalene is the first to witness the risen Jesus. She comes very early to Jesus' tomb and cries. Let us think for a moment about Mary's tears. This woman is very distressed. She lets her tears flow; she does not stop herself from expressing her suffering. And Jesus appears to her. She will recognize Him only when she hears her name. She turns around, experiences a real change of heart, and sees her Savior, whom she could not recognize just before that. Then Jesus asks her to announce His Resurrection to His brothers, who do not yet know what has happened, "Go to my brethren and say to them, I am ascending to my Father and your Father, to my God and your God." And Mary spreads the Good News.

This woman is given the task of bringing hope where there is none and bringing light into the night in which the disciples have been steeped for three days. As women, we are also called to be witnesses of Jesus' Resurrection and to announce it. The first ones to be affected are our families, especially our children. How many children recall the way in which their mothers spoke of Jesus with tenderness and simplicity? These are moments that have helped the faith of many people. Father Marcel Jousse remembers that his mother, who was illiterate, sang Bible passages while rocking him. He was soothed by the Word of God while being rocked. Let us sing, pray, and speak the Word to our children, even when they are newborns; may we not hesitate to announce the Good News to them with the simplicity of a mother who speaks and sings to her child.

Certain mothers also like to meet in a prayer group for mothers, which meets once a week, to pray for their children and support each other. The founder of this movement, which is now international, had started with this word, "Pray for your children." And what miracles have occurred as a result of prayer coming from the hearts of mothers!

God, who also has this heart of mercy, hears us. Whatever our denomination, let us dare to pray together for our children. This initiative is a source of blessings and helps us recall that God is in charge of everything and that our children are, above all, His children.

The mother also has an important role to play in words of blessing that are pronounced over her children. All during their growth, we can bless our children and tell them again that they are loved by God. The word "benediction" comes from the Latin *benedicere*, which means " to say good things." We are called to say good things about our child. Let us be attentive to what comes out of our mouths, "Set a guard over my mouth, O LORD; keep watch over the door of my lips" (Ps. 141:3). May we know how to ask for forgiveness and bless each other.

The role of the mother is not exclusive to her, of course, for the Word is transmitted by two people, and it is important that the father participate in this transmission. Generally, he is the one who transmits words of the outer world—such as those having to do with the law and rules—whereas the woman transmits words of the inner world—such as those dealing with spirituality and one's interior life. She is the one who, at night, will offer hope. If she gives up, it is possible that everything will crumble. Let us recall Mary, the Mother of Jesus, who carried the Word in her. The woman is the bearer and guardian of the Word, like Mary. Because of her welcoming and giving nature, she is able to give God to children.

It is possible that some women sometimes find it difficult to become mothers or to be women. Not everything is innate, and this strongly depends on what each one has gone through. Also, the experience of her own birth, as it was undergone by her mother, is significant, and it is important to be able to relive these moments to be aware of any possible wounds. Mary cries. And Jesus is not insensitive to our pains. On the contrary, He takes them on Himself. We can relive these moments by ourselves, on a retreat, or with a spiritual companion who allows us to see how the Holy Spirit is acting in our lives and helps us to get closer to Jesus and go step by step on the path of His Word. Let us ask the Lord to be able to experience our femininity as a gift from Him and to receive from Him this motherhood, which is the herald of life and hope.

*For Further Reflection*

We can complete our meditation with the text in which Hannah offers the gift of the one who is dearest to her, her son Samuel, giving him completely to God (1 Sam. 1:21–28). We can continue by observing what Samuel becomes: "As Samuel grew up, the LORD was with him and let none of his words fall to the ground" (1 Sam. 3:19). Regarding Hannah, his mother, "And the LORD took note of Hannah; she conceived and bore three sons and two daughters. And the boy Samuel grew up in the presence of the LORD" (1 Sam. 2:21).

So, we see how grace overflowed for Hannah, much more than what she expected.

## A Concluding Prayer

*Lord Jesus, You who showed Yourself to Mary Magdalene in front of the tomb, called her by her first name, and entrusted her to announce the Good News of the Resurrection to the disciples, help me to announce the Word to my children lovingly and tenderly. Inspire me with prayers and words of blessing and lullabies that speak of You. Work in my children and help them to persevere in prayer. Heal that which is scarred and wounded in me, and may I be able, like Mary, Your Mother, to feel the joy of the Resurrection. May I be aware of the beauty of my vocation as a woman, a wife, and a mother. Amen.*

# The Ending Word

Here is, as a conclusion, the ten-point postpartum guide to help you survive the first months after childbirth, when discouragement shows up, accompanied by extreme fatigue:

1. Be gentle with yourself.

2. Be merciful toward yourself, and know how to forgive yourself.

3. Recall this: your children are, first, the Lord's. He watches over them.

4. Try to be joyous: "Joy is the remedy for fatigue, which causes discouragement (Saint Seraphim of Sarov).

5. In every moment, ask for the grace to accept your reality today.

6. Tell your husband at least once a day that you love him, and do something to show this to him.

7. Each day, spend time exclusively with your baby so that you may get to know each other through skin-to-skin contact, massage, a baby carrier, or a lullaby.

8. Do only one thing at a time without thinking of all those things that are waiting to be done.

9. Be helped by people of goodwill.

10. Meditate on this text from 1 Kings 19:3–9, when the prophet Elijah is nourished by an angel under the broom tree as he wants to die, "Arise and eat, else the journey will be too great for you."

# Notes

# Notes

# Notes

# Notes

# Notes

# Notes

# Notes

# Notes

# Sophia Institute

Sophia Institute is a nonprofit institution that seeks to nurture the spiritual, moral, and cultural life of souls and to spread the Gospel of Christ in conformity with the authentic teachings of the Roman Catholic Church.

Sophia Institute Press fulfills this mission by offering translations, reprints, and new publications that afford readers a rich source of the enduring wisdom of mankind.

Sophia Institute also operates two popular online Catholic resources: CrisisMagazine.com and CatholicExchange.com.

*Crisis Magazine* provides insightful cultural analysis that arms readers with the arguments necessary for navigating the ideological and theological minefields of the day. *Catholic Exchange* provides world news from a Catholic perspective as well as daily devotionals and articles that will help you to grow in holiness and live a life consistent with the teachings of the Church.

In 2013, Sophia Institute launched Sophia Institute for Teachers to renew and rebuild Catholic culture through service to Catholic education. With the goal of nurturing the spiritual, moral, and cultural life of souls, and an abiding respect for the role and work of teachers, we strive to provide materials and programs that are at once enlightening to the mind and ennobling to the heart; faithful and complete, as well as useful and practical.

Sophia Institute gratefully recognizes the Solidarity Association for preserving and encouraging the growth of our apostolate over the course of many years. Without their generous and timely support, this book would not be in your hands.

www.SophiaInstitute.com
www.CatholicExchange.com
www.CrisisMagazine.com
www.SophiaInstituteforTeachers.org